Black Bone:

Poems on Crime and Punishment, Race and Justice

Black Bone:

Poems on Crime and Punishment, Race and Justice

Poems by Alexa Marie Kelly

Cover Art by Rachel Ternes
Cover Design by Carla Mavaddat
Text Design by Sonia Tabriz

BleakHouse Publishing
2015

Bleakhouse Publishing

Ward Circle Building 254
American University
Washington, DC 20016

NEC Box 67
New England College
Henniker, New Hampshire 03242

www.BleakHousePublishing.com

Robert Johnson – Editor & Publisher
Sonia Tabriz - Managing Editor
Liz Calka - Creative Director

Casey Chiappetta - Marketing Director
Shirin Karimi - Senior Creative Consultant
Carla Mavaddat – Art Director

Joanna Heaney – Chief Operations Officer
Alexa Marie Kelly – Chief Editorial Officer
Nora Kirk – Chief Development Officer
Rachel Ternes – Chief Creative Officer

ISBN-13: 978-0-9837769-9-4

Printed in the United States of America

To Mom, Dad and Jack

Table of Contents

Acknowledgments

I would not be who I am today without Professor Robert Johnson. His Deprivation of Liberty class changed my life. It opened my heart to entire populations of people devastated by our criminal justice system.

BleakHouse Publishing would not exist without the energy and compassion of Professor Johnson. He motivates some of American University's brightest students to write, to empathize, and to create beautiful books.

I'd of course like to thank Professor Johnson for always believing in my poetry. For honoring me with the BleakHouse Fellowship. For brining unheard voices onto paper with countless published poems on prisoners, death row inmates and the inherent humanity we all share.

Black Bone

Tickets rain down
Like dead confetti.
Blue slips, court dates.
We slip, life waits.
We are the hunted.
Stalked on street-corners
We slink, they cuff.
Cold steel on bone.
Lock us up.
Take our home
For an open bottle
An afternoon buzz.
They watch us squirm.
They eat our pain.
We are hungry,
Flightless birds.
But
Youthful stupidity looks
Better on white skin.
Light slaps
For the rich.
For us it's
Cold steel on black bone.

Ferguson

What happens to a boy deferred?
He festers in the sun.
A ribbon of blood drains from
The six bullet holes pierced in his dark skin,
His soft face pushed flat on asphalt.
A heavy load not carried,
Rotting in the spotlight.
A warning to his friends
This could be you.

Frankenstein

I am the scary monster
Torn from the father's mind

Dead eyes stare from the daughter
You teach her to
Look away
Hold her breath
Clench her fist

Believe myths of hooded figures
Who snatch her in the night

Black skin devils who rape and kill
And burn

There's science fiction to your
Stories

Sins of the Father

Father
grease in his nails
creak in his neck
ache in his bones

faded gray jumpsuit
stained with sweat and oil
wrench worn with rust

breaks his back to
keep his son
away from the blacks

Son
baggy jeans weighed
down with loose change
and scraps of poetry

adderall-induced nightmares
of apple pie and
wooden Sunday church pews

bears his cross to
absolve our sins and
save the blacks

Write Your Name

across my chest etched
in stretch marks and long nights
are the times i held you
baby boy,
you are lucky, my son
grown with books piled high
and ink-stained fingers
long nights, big glasses and
words
write your dreams, son
breathe in old books
because i hold your library card,
wear the white plastic down between
my palms
trace my finger over your signature
write your name, son
don't let them take
your words.

I let my Brother go

I let my brother go
Not because he was the better man
(He wasn't.)
I let my brother go
Not because I am clean
(I'm not.)
I let my brother go
Because I love.
I let my brother go
Because I see in his
Newborn eyes not a
Hardness nor a
Disease but the divine
Light of the Lord.
I let my brother go.

The Man he Killed

The man he killed will never
Drink instant coffee
Lose at chess
Teach a class
Learn a lesson
Mentor a drug addict
Publish a book
Call home
Argue
Fight
Cry
Piss off prison guards
Appreciate solitude
Feel loved or missed or lonely
Feel tired or torn or dead
(Maybe dead.)
But never indignant and never
Helpless
He will not be a lawyer or
A janitor
He will not be a clerk
Or a hero
He will just be
Dead.

That Only Happens in California

That only happens in California
Overcrowded, filthy and dark
Cells for men.
Caged.
Tightly coiled dust
Forgotten when the wind blows
Medicated within an inch of
What could be called "lives"
My backyard is clear
My backyard is clean
Repeat, repeat, repeat
We see shadows of truth
We will know blindness
I do not want to believe
That my neighbors are dying
Trapped dust in ugly cells
Locked in gang wars
Suffocating
That does not happen here
That does happen, hear.
This misery cannot be so close
To home

A Prisoner's Body

If a surgeon took
His scalpel to me
No soot would escape

I bleed in red

Beneath my matted hair
Twisted and broken now from lack
Of affection

No horns grow

I am a sinner and
My soul is not clean
But

I bruise in deep purple
Just like you.

Painted Man

In my life I painted houses
Dripped color on clean walls

I trace the battle scar that spans my stomach
A thick brown reminder

A fault line that aches and squirms and cracks
When the sun hides

The strip of sweat-soaked cotton
Wrung around my neck

They slashed my noose and
I fell
Bloodied knuckles and knotted insides

They gripped my wrist and dragged my chains
Concrete on skin
Inflamed bowels and shattered eyes

In my cell they painted me
My brown scar

Without Color

In me there was an artist.
In me there was the sun.
The caged heart has no mornings.
Only lifeless dusk.
I cannot paint without color.
You see, the artist died
When I killed her.
Prison took what remained of my soul.
To pass the seconds to eternity
We etch nonsense into cell walls.
Scratch with fingernails
Smear blood or shit.
The only art that's left.

Bathroom Marks

scrawled in thin ink across the concrete wall
meant to trigger
meant to damage

a five-letter reminder
that you are less than a man

shame bubbles beneath your hot skin
you trace the bruise across your neck

"whore"

A Winter's Tale

The surface of my eyeball brims wet
from the ice-cold breeze that
whips my skin as
snot drips from my nostrils

Barbed-wire cuts the blue sky
above my shaking frame
Graying guards shove their fists
deep into their khakis to keep warm

But still I stand on the rough concrete patch
I raise my cracked, black hands to the heavens
Fresh air tastes so much better than prison

All There Is

Sweet talk to me.
Tell me all there is
On the other side
Of the sun.

Break bread with me.
For tomorrow there is
More
Of the same.

There was:

Slow dance,
Strawberry jam and
Sweet talks.

There is

a cell now.

I Dream of Hands

I dream of hands.
Supple palms unclenched
And open and warm.
Interlaced fingers in
A dark theater, buttery from popcorn
And soft to touch.
Dream hands to brush back my hair.
Hands to hold my waist.
I wake to my nightmare.
My hands are dry,
Cracked and bloody in winter
Because the notion
Of giving hand-cream to prisoners is
Ridiculous.
No one will hold my hand anyway.

Homeward Bound

Homeward bound but
Bound to fall

Where to go
And what to ask

Cycles of sin
Circle the center of me

Let me go.
Let me live.

Free, free and fated
For what?

Exonerated

I wipe my mouth on my sleeve
Salty with sweat and gin
I grasp the bottle
Hold it close like a child

I still see the
Cold florescent light
Underneath my eyelids

I still feel the
Torn skin on my ankles

The indignant cuts from
Steel cuffs
Left purple scars around my wrists

Freedom never felt so much like prison.

Old Man Killer

Old Man Killer
I did not think you would be old.
But there you are,
Like my grandfather before he passed,
A man with sagging skin.
Nothing but time and prison bars and godless nights
Behind your diamond eyes.
Where are you, killer?
Where are you, thug?
Could you still pull that trigger?
Spill his blood, bury his bones,
Beneath that unforgiving highway?
Or have your hands gone limp, weary, dead?
No, I don't think you could kill.
We kept you caged so long that you
Forgot how to fight
How to eat, how to cry.
You could not hurt me.
I know.

How I feel about the Death Penalty on a Gut Level

You raped and killed a five-year-old girl.
I would kill you myself.

Last Meal

We are made of bone
Pulled from the side
of a holy man
come undone
by woman and fruit
and promise.
-

Grease cloaks my fingers
like fog on a Sunday sky.
Cracking rib without grace,
I peel back layers of skin,
my teeth dusted black.
-

I am the cannibal
you want me to be
-

Spare my bones.

Electric Chair Lullaby

Oh momma won't you plant me a cherry tree?
That's where I'll go when they come for me.
Hey brother won't you buy me a getaway car?
We'll hope right in, and we'll go real far.
Oh sister won't you bake me a birthday cake?
That's what I'll eat before the pearly gates.
Hey papa won't you swing me a wedding dance?
That's what I want; I want a second chance.
Oh stranger won't you smile me a friendly stare?
When you guide me down to that final chair.
Hey sinner won't you find me some God today?
Plug me in, and I'll be on my way.

To Kill a Phoenix

I feel my body burning
Blister my fingertips
Pop open the nerve endings

From the tip of your needle
To the top of my spine
I breathe the fire

Inferno, my friend
Towering flames to the ash
My body blackens deep, dark, dust

Lethal, your injection
But to conquer the Phoenix
You need more than a burn

Body and Soul

he warned me not to notice when the soul left the body but i
saw its gray spirit leave the gentle devil man he killed and he
lost he was beaten and they dreamed that one day his victims
would find peace in his decay i traveled to where his soul
trembled by the window seeking freedom from the
deathroom to find God in his kingdom i set free the breath
of his afterlife i wish i could die too i brought the mothers
flowers both childless both alone we would stand there in the
silence that watches over still bones i would miss my
tortured brother not of blood but of flesh and heart and God
really i forgive you brother or i want because you were a lost
child and you told me you found grace on sunday mornings
when the sunlight touched your cage i told you i loved dust
that dances in the rays we laughed and talked of mornings
but you lost your sunrises when you choked my baby sister
till she died till she was dead still i'm sorry to see you go my
sister's killer my true friend.

The Innocent

We just sucked out all the poison
From the man who would not win.
There was pain we could not succor
There was time and there was sin.
He forgave us for our trespasses.
He committed none we saw.
We killed him to forget him.
He saves us one and all.
In my life I'll be a Quaker
Fill my days with soft and peace.
The gurney or the crucifix,
Which will help us better sleep?
Convicted demon, damned prophet
There is innocence in faith.
There are no atheists in the death house
Only beggars, prayers, and grace.

[handwritten margin note: Mayella sined religion & church importance]

The Mourning After

I see his reflection in my morning coffee. He seeps into my day, settles in like a thick smell. His shadow stalks my shallow steps. The warden chants in my ear, "Call it killin, call it executin, call it whatever you'd like. The man dies anyway." Call me killer. Executioner, executing justice for you, for us, for our need to purge the world of numb hearts and rotting minds. What of my mind? What of my immortal soul? Each life taken is an ink-stain, black like the coffee, black like his skin and black like the barrel of his gun. Its shaking bullets pierced that poor child seventeen times. Deader than he'll ever be. Deader, even, than my eyes on this bastardized morning after. A hangover with all of the headache and none of the hazy pleasure. No girl in my bed. Only his phantom in my eyes.

Charon

He protects convicted killers
because he doesn't want them to
die alone.
But
Her life runs parallel
Rarely crossing, never conjoined
to his.
He finds grace and honor
in the men he tries to save,
As his young son watches
Spongebob, alone in the suburbs.
His line of work seeps into
His son's nightmares
Every execution is
a pained scream from his small frame.
He deals in life and death
In wasted time, wasted lives
Too guilty to continue and
too unholy to quit.
This business of execution
Of lost nights, missed snow cones,
Of men dead before we kill them
Of his wife walking the winter beach alone
Of shuttering like Charon
This business of defending the condemned
is killing him.

About the Author

ALEXA MARIE KELLY will graduate from the American University honors program in May 2015, with a degree in public relations, marketing and literature. BleakHouse Publishing has shaped Kelly's undergraduate experience. It inspired her to co-lead an alternative break trip to San Francisco, to study prison reform. As 2014 and 2015 Editor-in-Chief of Tacenda Literary Magazine, Kelly worked to publish incarcerated writers and AU students alike. Kelly also manages submissions to BleakHouse as its chief-editorial-officer. She became BleakHouse Fellow in 2014, joining a legacy of talented, engaged poets. Kelly is honored to have worked with Professor Robert Johnson every step of the way.

About the Artist and Designers

CARLA MAVADDAT is a graduate of McGill University with a passion for photography and design. She is originally from Montreal, Canada, but grew up in Washington, DC. Carla is interested in human rights, in social justice, and is a strong advocate against poverty. Her photos have appeared in Adore Noir, among other venues. Mavaddat is the graphics and design editor for BleakHouse Review.

SONIA TABRIZ graduated from American University (2010) *summa cum laude* with University Honors, with a B.A. in Law & Society and Psychology. She received the Outstanding Scholarship at the Undergraduate Level award for her award-winning works of fiction, legal commentaries, artwork, presentations, university-wide accolades, and academic achievement. Tabriz went on to attend The George Washington University Law School, where she served as a Writing Fellow and Editor-in-Chief of the *Public Contract Law Journal*. She is now an attorney in the Washington, DC office of a national law firm. Tabriz is the Managing Editor of BleakHouse Publishing and designs the text for various publications.

RACHEL TERNES is an honors undergraduate student at American University majoring in psychology and minoring in French and studio arts. Her passion for creating art is rivaled only by her interest in using her artistic skill to promote causes of social justice. As Chief Creative Officer for BleakHouse Publishing, Ternes designs visuals for the press releases and publicity, and contributes to the visual design and illustration of publications.

Other Titles from BleakHouse Publishing

An Elegy for Old Terrors, Zoé Orfanos

Up the River, Chandra Bozelko

Distant Thunder, Charles Huckelbury

Enclosures: Reflections from the Prison Cell and the Hospital Bed, Shirin Karimi

A Zoo Near You, Robert Johnson et al.

Origami Heart: Poems by a Woman Doing Life, Erin George

Tales from the Purple Penguin, Charles Huckelbury

Burnt Offerings, Robert Johnson

More Praise for *Black Bone*

From skin color and coffee grounds to the title poem, Kelly explores the darkest shades of guilt and innocence. *Black Bone* dives into the details, bringing the reader into a universe of "sweat-soaked cotton" and "teeth dusted black." Kelly's unflinching look at men and women on the outskirts of society lends strength to her book's vital message: "don't let them take your words."

- Zoé Orfanos, Consulting Editor of BleakHouse Publishing, author of *An Elegy for Old Terrors*

Alexa Marie Kelly's new book of poems puts to rest any delusions about race in America, especially with respect to the criminal justice system. She masters the difficult challenge of capturing imprisonment, including executions and suicides, from an exclusively free perspective. Few outsiders can understand a life in which the man or woman never feels safe anywhere, but Kelly eloquently describes it: "The caged heart has no mornings."

In a nod to Langston Hughes, she reminds us that a dream or a boy deferred must both confront the same obstacles, demonstrating that nothing significant has changed in nearly a hundred years. Indeed, in her poem "Frankenstein" we hear echoes of the Civil War canard regarding the predatory nature of black men in their pursuit of white women. And, sadly, as Kelly points out in another poem, it doesn't "happen only in California."

Alexa Kelly has given us something disturbing but also necessary if this country is ever to move into a post-racial society and leave behind the perpetual long, dark night of a criminal justice system that values money and power over the individual. It is a tonic to the misinformation one hears during the unending election cycles and a volume that should be on any thinking person's shopping list.

- Charles Huckelbury, Senior Consulting Editor of BleakHouse Publishing, award-winning poet and author of *Tales from the Purple Penguin* and *Distant Thunder*

Black Bone is a brave and astute commentary narrated in eloquent verse. Through Kelly's voice, we hear the passionate laments of condemned characters who we recognize through the lens of history. The prisoner, the executioner, and the exonerated are allowed to speak freely and we in turn are free to acknowledge their submerged "prayers and grace" in the darkness of our justice system.

- Shirin Karimi, Senior Creative Consultant of BleakHouse Publishing, and author of award-winning book, *Enclosures*

9 780983 776994